Math in Focus

Singapore Math®
by Marshall Cavendish®

M000009462

GRADE
KA

Student Book
Part 1

Author
Dr. Pamela Sharpe

U.S. Consultants
Andy Clark
Patsy F. Kanter

 **Marshall Cavendish**
Education

U.S. Distributor

**Houghton
Mifflin
Harcourt**

© 2018 Marshall Cavendish Education Pte Ltd

Published by Marshall Cavendish Education
Times Centre, 1 New Industrial Road, Singapore 536196
Customer Service Hotline: (65) 6213 9688
US Office Tel: (1-914) 332 8888 | Fax: (1-914) 332 8882
E-mail: cs@mceducation.com
Website: www.mceducation.com

Distributed by
Houghton Mifflin Harcourt
222 Berkeley Street
Boston, MA 02116
Tel: 617-351-5000
Website: www.hmheducation.com/mathinfocus

Cover: © Bob Elsdale/Eureka/Alamy.
Image provided by Houghton Mifflin Harcourt.

First published 2018

ISBN 978-1-328-88057-4

Printed in Singapore

7 8 9 10   1401   24 23 22 21 20
4500814554   A B C D E

Contents

Chapter 1 Numbers to 5

Lesson 1 All About 1 and 2

Recite.

Two big potatoes met in a lane,
Bowed most politely, bowed once again.
How do you do? How do you do?
How do you do again?

Two tall green beans met in a lane,
Bowed most politely, bowed once again.
How do you do? How do you do?
How do you do again?

Match.

Trace.

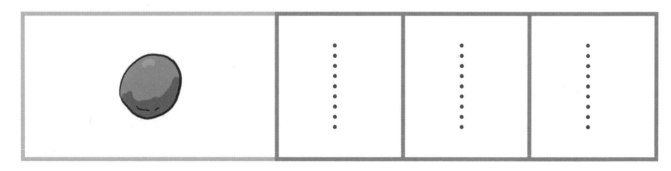

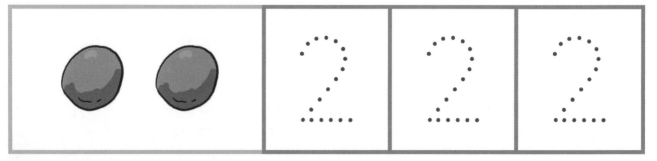

Count and write.

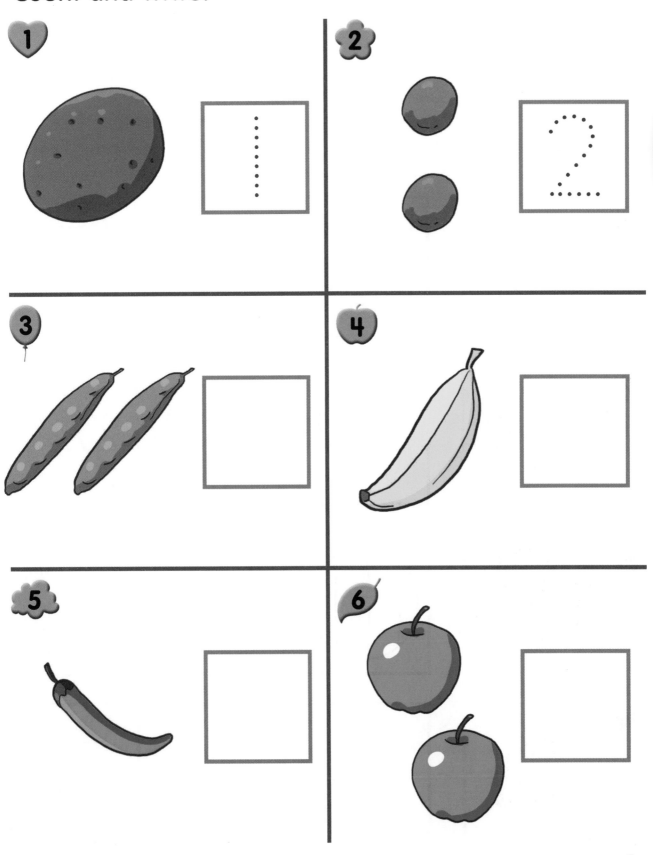

Lesson 2 Finding Matches
Color the same object.

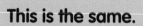

 This is the same.

 1

 2

 3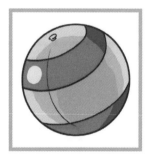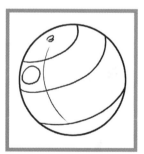

 4

Circle the groups of 2.

Draw the same object.

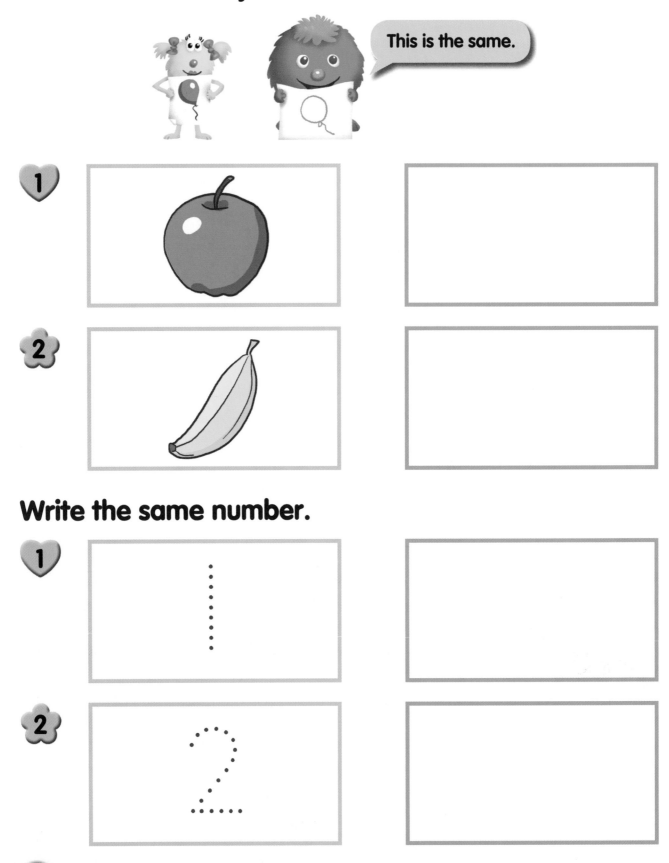

This is the same.

1 [apple illustration]

2 [banana illustration]

Write the same number.

1 1

2 2

Draw an object that is not the same.

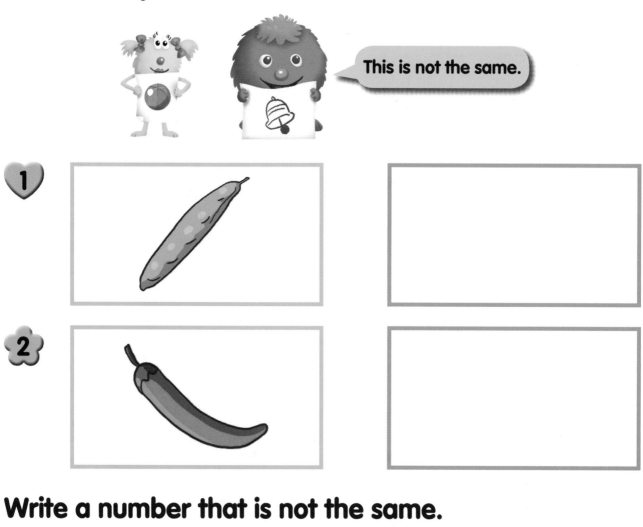

This is not the same.

Write a number that is not the same.

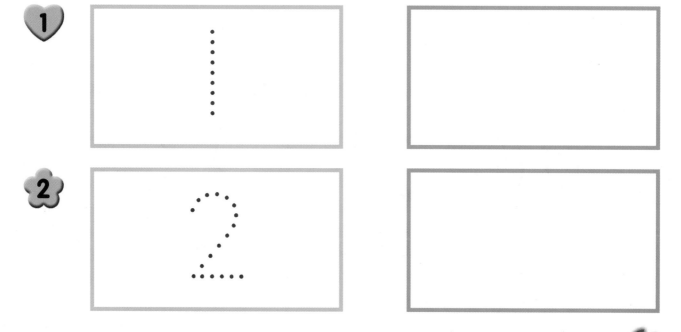

Match.

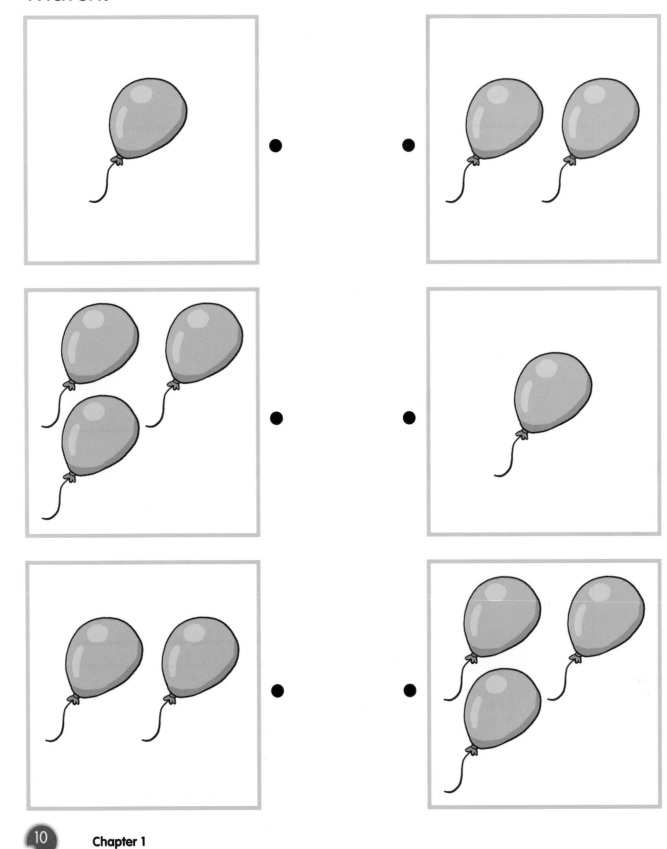

Trace.

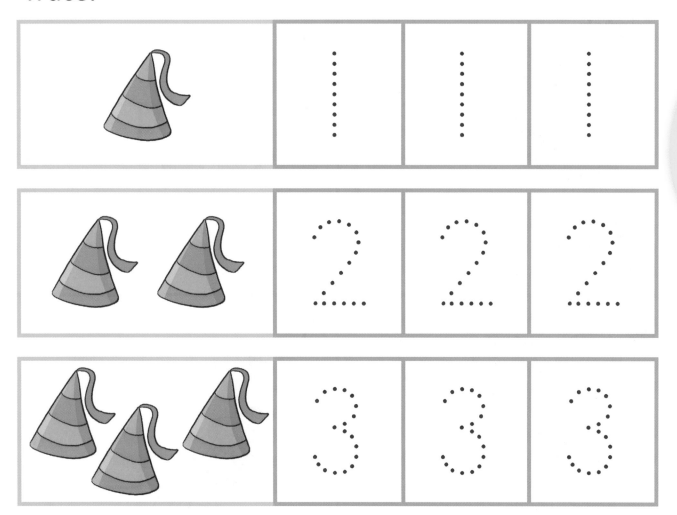

Look and say.

Count and write.

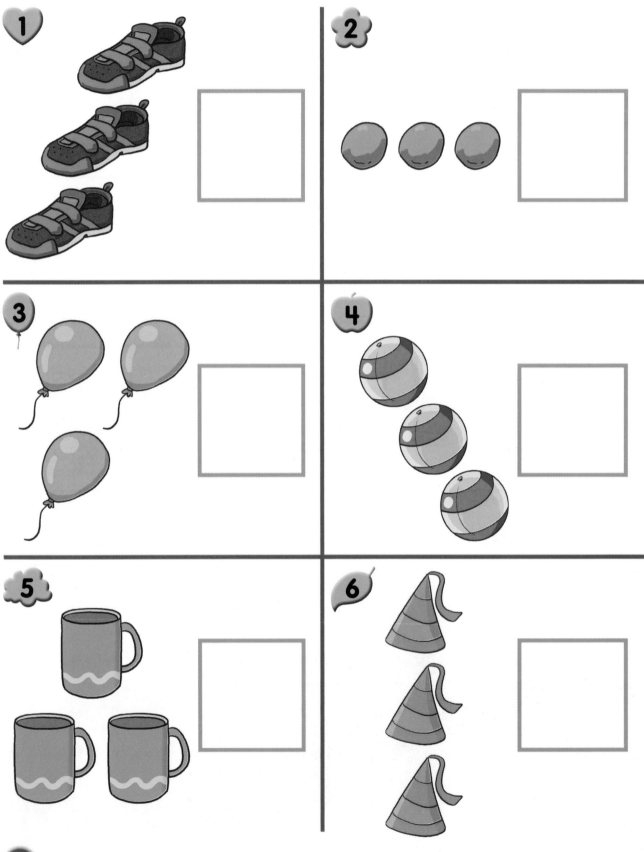

Look and say.

Match.

 ● ●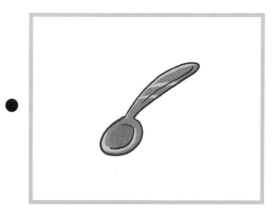

 ● ●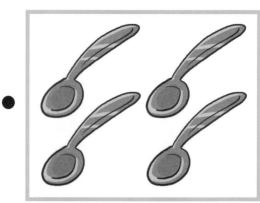

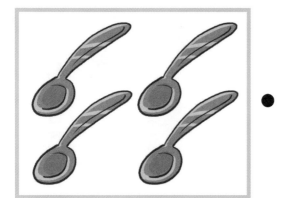 ● ●

 ● ●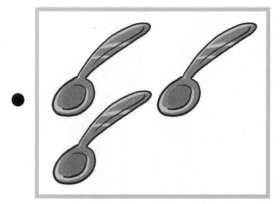

Trace.

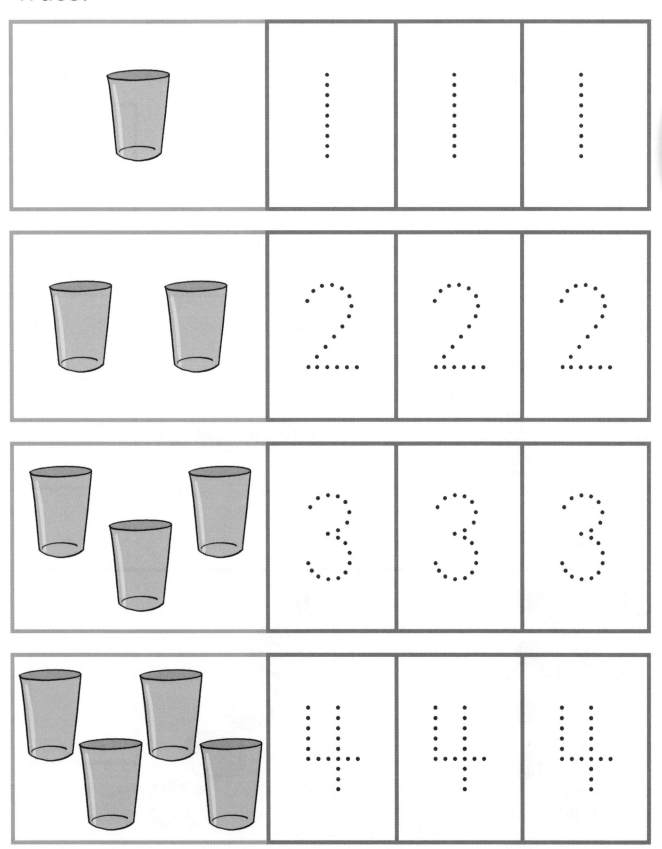

Count and write.

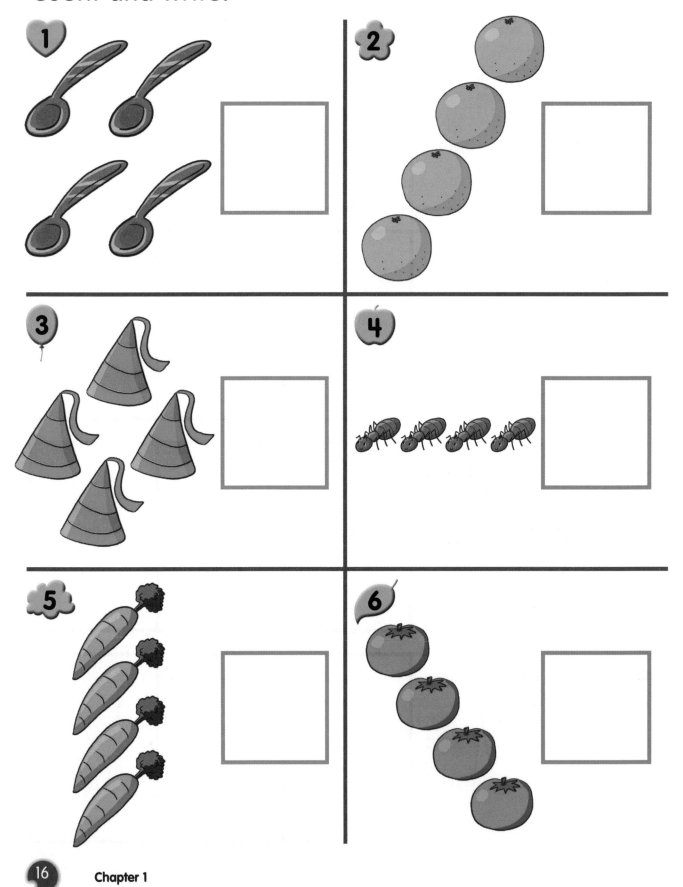

Look and win.

Look at the picture your teacher is holding up.

Look and say.

Draw a pretend animal.

My animal has ...

Match.

 • •

 • •

 • •

 • •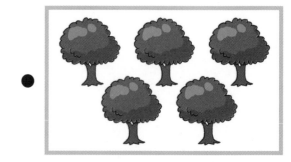

 • •

Trace.

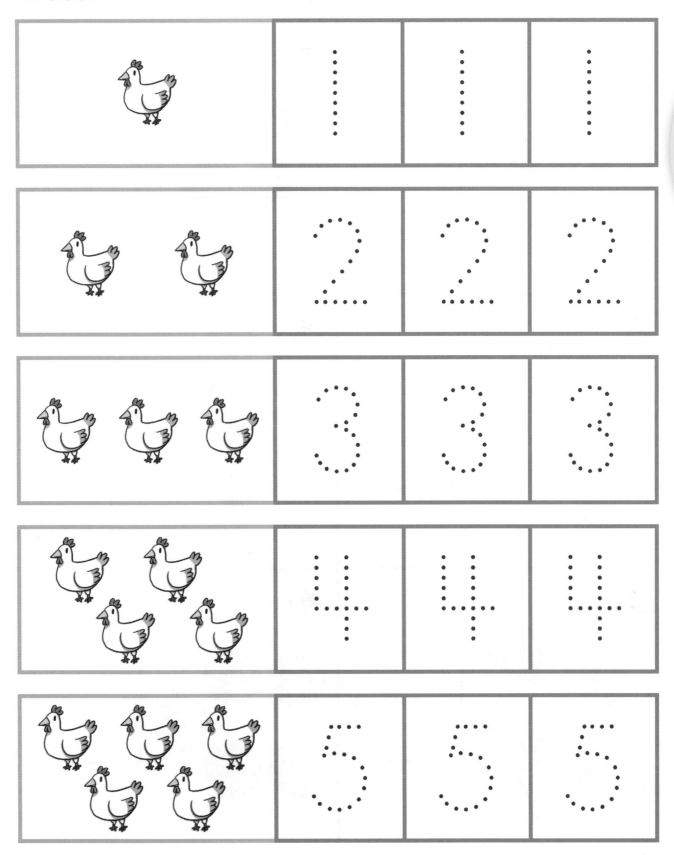

Count and write.

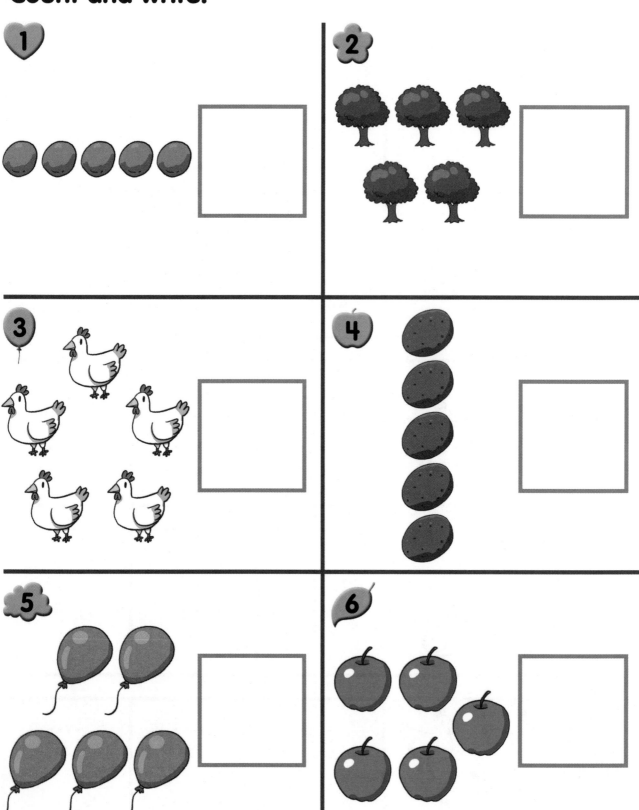

Lesson 6 Spotting Small Differences
Color 5 differences.

Circle the differences.

What is different?

things are different!

Lesson 1 All About 6

Match.

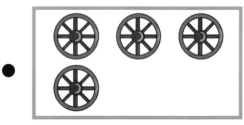

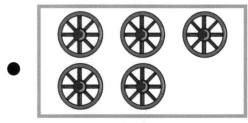

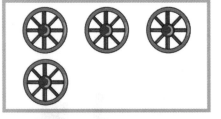

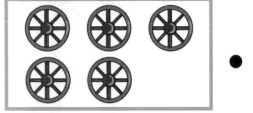

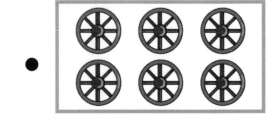

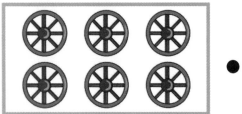

Draw.

Trace.

🚩	1	1	1
🚩🚩	2	2	2
🚩🚩🚩	3	3	3
🚩🚩🚩🚩	4	4	4
🚩🚩🚩🚩🚩	5	5	5
🚩🚩🚩🚩🚩🚩	6	6	6

Count and write.

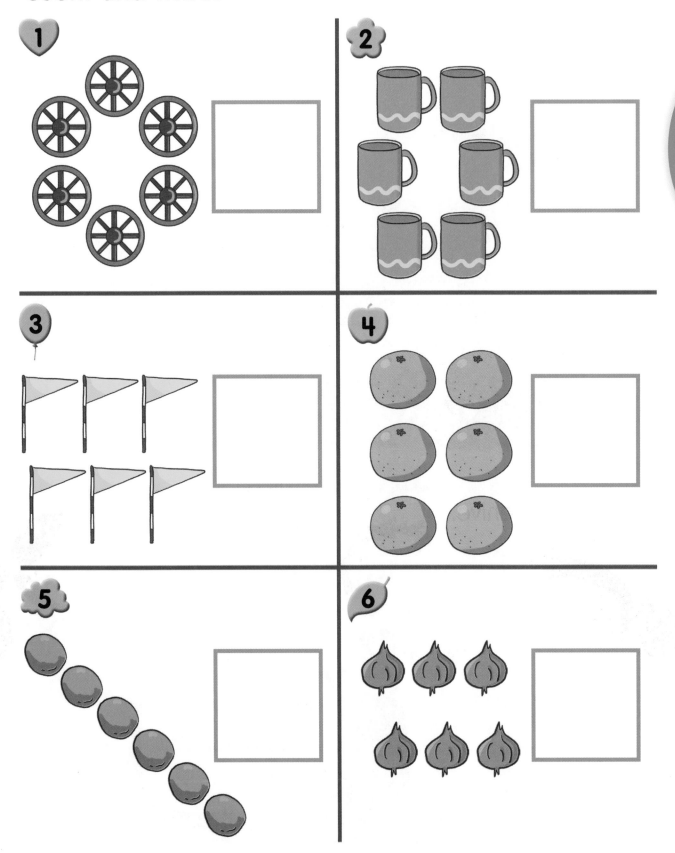

Sing.

Here is the beehive.

Where are the bees?

Hidden away where nobody sees.

Circle the groups of seven bees.

Match.

   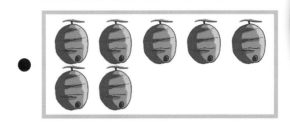

Draw.

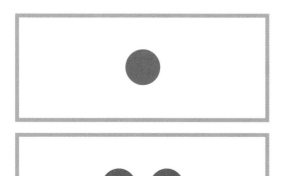

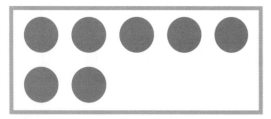

Trace.

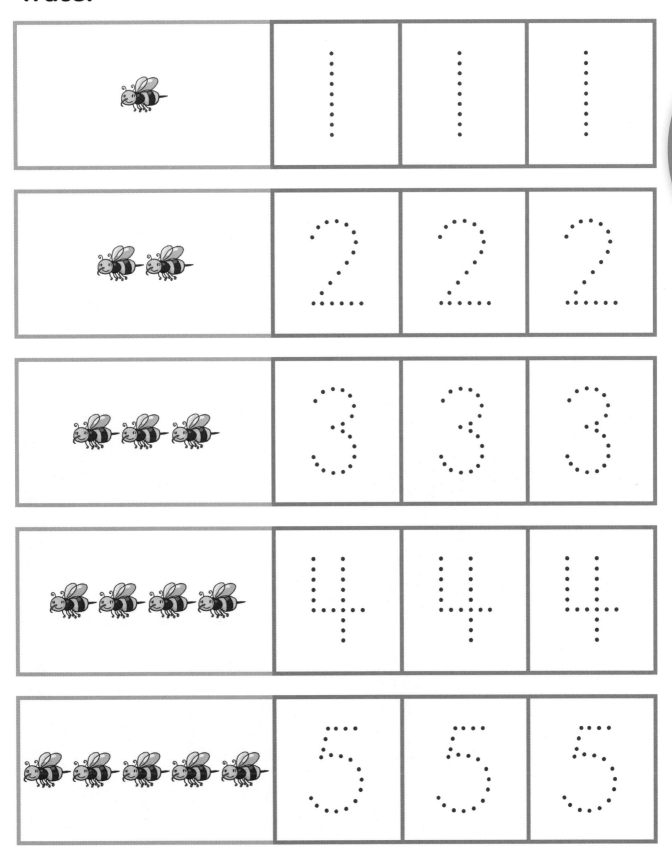

Trace.

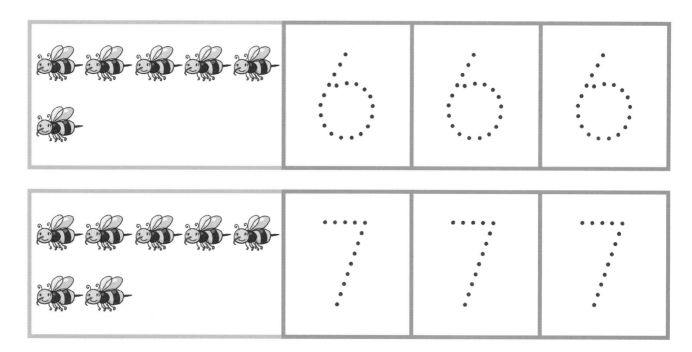

Look and say.

Count and write.

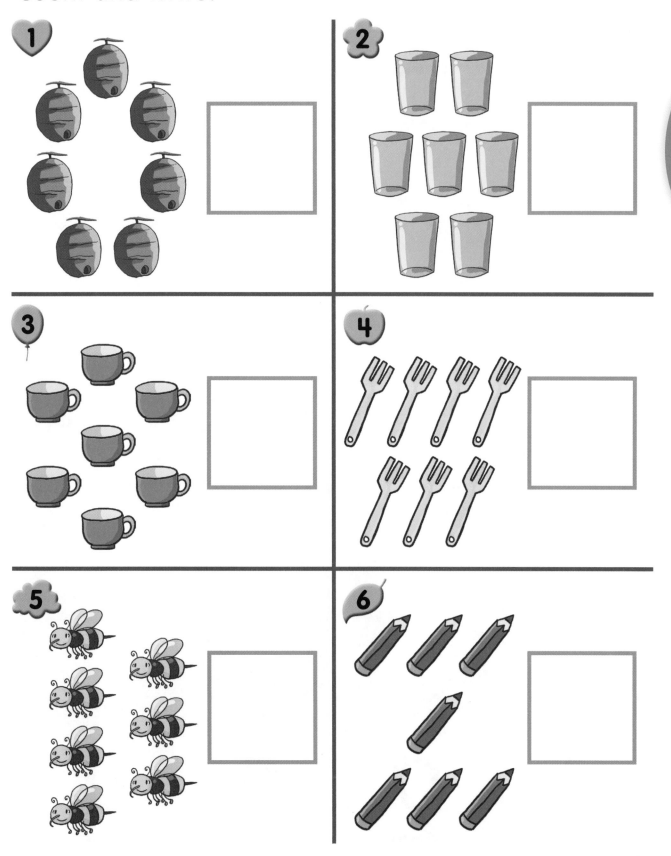

Color.

1 2 3 4

5   6   7   8

Draw.

Match.

 • •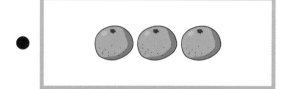

 • •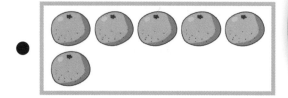

 • •

 • •

 • •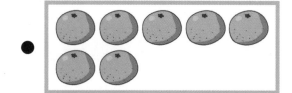

 • •

 • •

 • •

Draw.

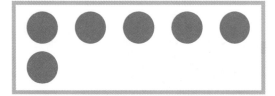

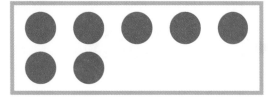

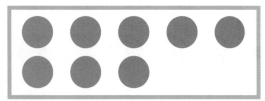

Trace.

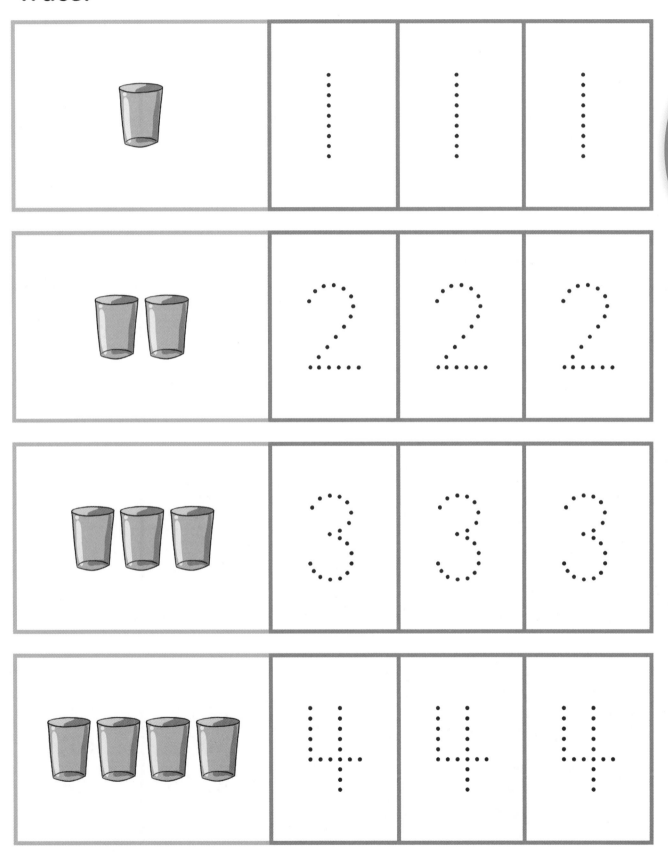

Trace.

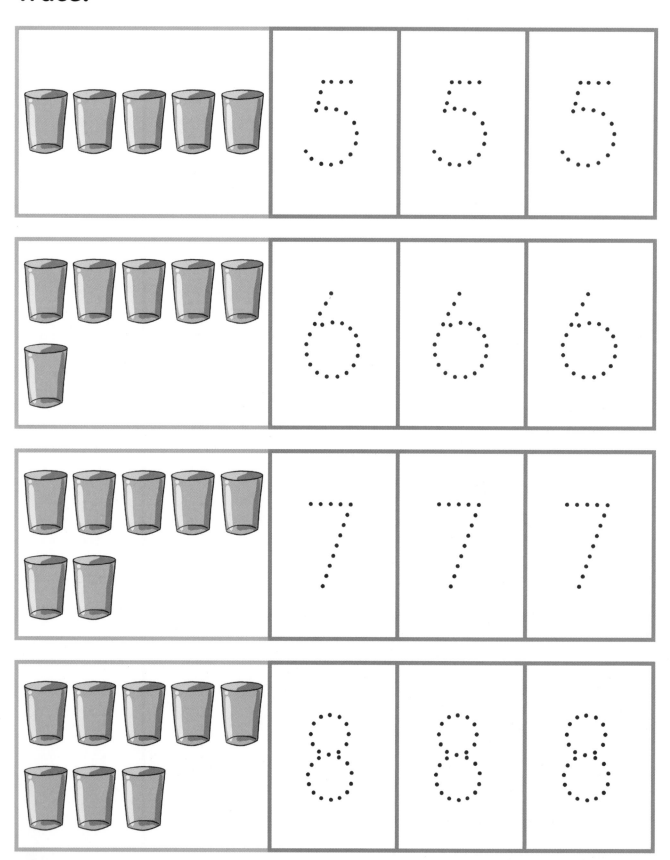

Count and write.

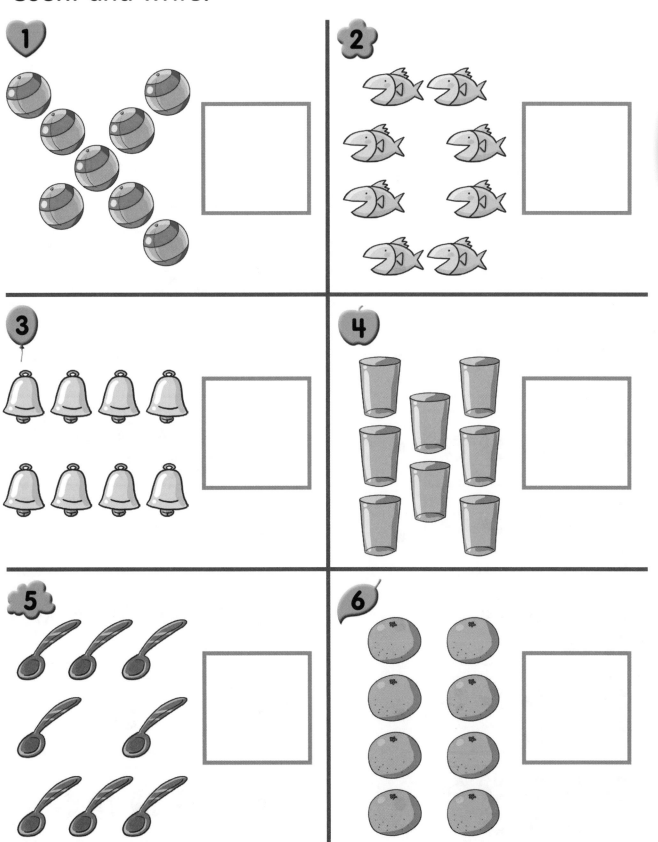

Match.

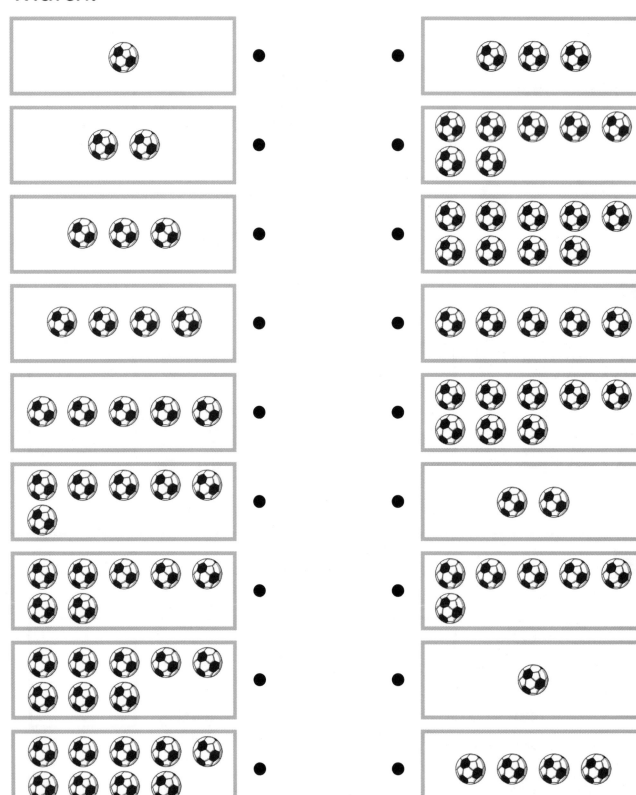

Draw.

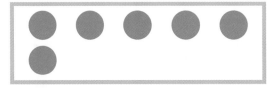

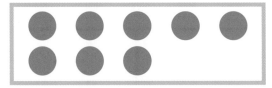

Trace.

	1	1	1
	2	2	2
	3	3	3
	4	4	4
	5	5	5

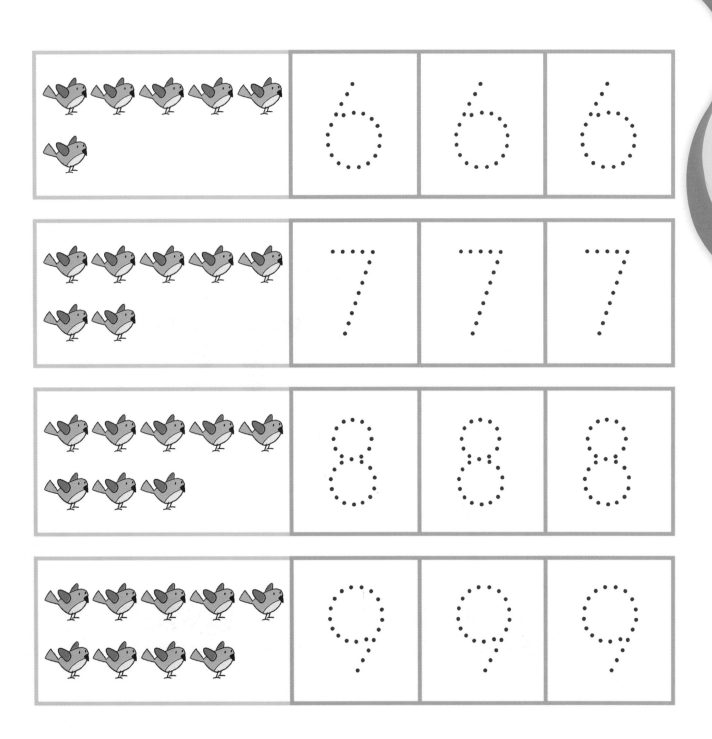

Write the missing numbers.

0   1   ☐   ☐   4

Count and write.

3

Count and write.

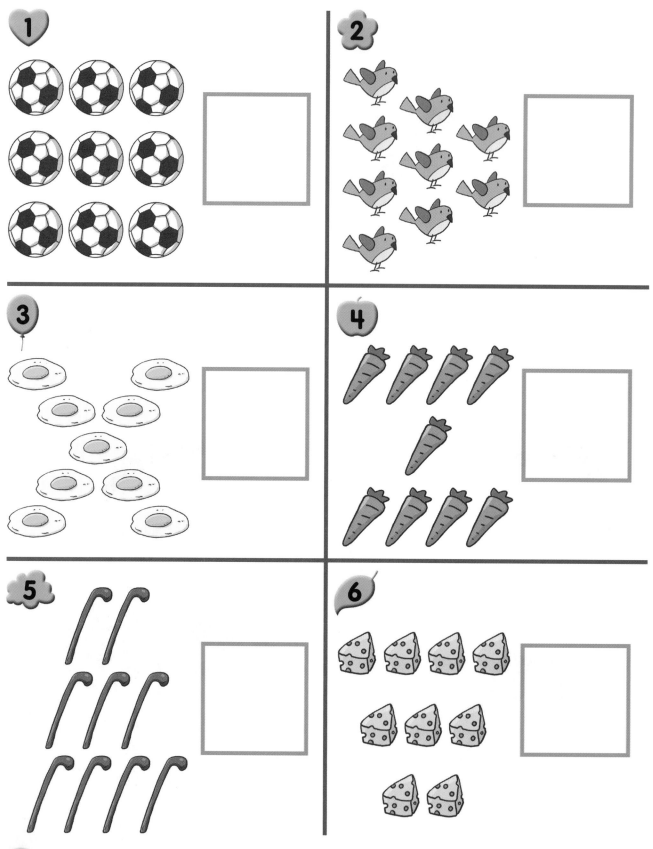

Lesson 6 Pairing One-to-One

What is missing?
Complete the set.

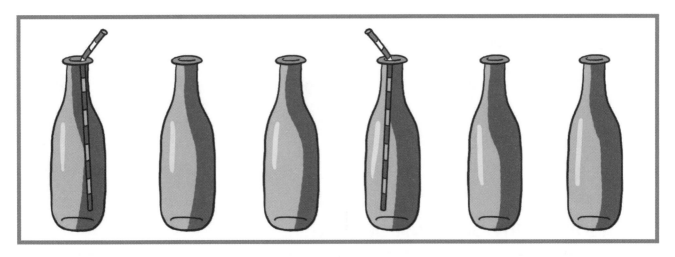

Circle, count, and write.

1 There is cheese for 6 mice.

How many mice will be hungry? _____

---

2 3 boys have coats.

How many boys will be cold? _____

---

3 There are 6 egg holders.

How many eggs are needed to fill all the egg holders? _____

Workmat **2**

WORK MAT

1	**2**
3	**4**

WORK MAT

Workmat 4